MAN-MADE WONDERS

BY CHARLOTTE EDWARDS

CONTENTS

Endpapers: The great stones of Stonehenge have stood on Salisbury Plain in England for over 4000 years.

Previous page: The steel 'Gateway to the West' Arch, in Missouri, is the tallest monument in the world; it is 192 metres (630 feet) high.

Left: The Cathedral of Notre Dame of Paris is one of the great Gothic cathedrals of Europe.

INTRODUCTION

From the earliest times, mankind has sought to dominate his environment and create permanent monuments of great beauty that would endure the passage of time. Throughout history, this challenge to Man's ingenuity has produced architectural achievements of such size and magnificence that they became regarded as objects of inspiration and wonderment.

It was the ancient Greeks who first expressed this sense of wonder by compiling the famous list of the *Seven Wonders of the World*: a catalogue of outstanding human accomplishments which has endured for centuries. The story of the Seven Wonders goes back to about the middle of the third century BC. The vast empire of Alexander the Great had broken up into a series of kingdoms which enjoyed a measure of peace and stability. Consequently, people were able to travel around fairly safely from country to country and see wondrous sights and exotic places. In Greece, guide books and travelogues became popular and the idea of tourism was established. From this interest in foreign travel grew the list of 'astounding sights' which came to be known as the Seven Wonders of the World. The original list has not been preserved and no less than 25 versions of it have come down to us from antiquity, but the general catalogue is as follows:

1 The Pyramids at Giza; 2 The Hanging Gardens of Babylon; 3 The Statue of Zeus at Olympia; 4 The Temple of Artemis at Ephesus; 5 The Mausoleum of Halicarnassus; 6 The Colossus of Rhodes; 7 The Pharos at Alexandria.

In later centuries there were many revisions and substitutions to this list. The Romans, for example, considered that their Colosseum rivalled the Colossus of Rhodes. The actual number of wonders always remained the same, however; the number seven held profound mystical meaning and magical powers for the ancient world and it appears frequently in early symbols and legends. Certainly the Greeks considered the Seven Wonders to be important; in their search for harmony and perfection they probably regarded a visit to one of the marvels more as a pilgrimage than a holiday trip.

Even today we are still inspired by the wonders of the past. Not only are we fascinated by the sheer size and often eerie beauty of surviving glories, we are amazed that such great feats of architecture could be created without modern equipment and technology.

Early builders and architects were able to solve the most complex problems with only the simplest of tools and techniques to help them. They were able to quarry huge blocks of stone merely by driving wooden wedges into specially chiselled slots. The wood was then saturated with water so that the pressure of the expanding wedges would split the rock. Stonemasons of centuries ago developed sophisticated techniques without metal tools to aid them. The Inca craftsmen of Macchu Picchu in South America fitted the stones of their buildings together with such precision that it is impossible, even today, to insert a knife blade between them.

Lack of powerful, wheeled vehicles did not prevent the transportation of vast loads over great distances, centuries ago. The Egyptians brought their huge stones down the Nile on rafts, and it is thought that the builders of Stonehenge in Wiltshire, England, may have used river and sea transport to bring some of their stones from South Wales. Transportation overland in ancient Egypt was sometimes achieved by soaking the soil to provide a slippery surface over which to slide the

---

The rich, ceramic decoration which covers the façade and minarets of this 15th-century tomb in Mahan, Iran (*right*) is a traditional feature of Islamic architecture. The use of enamelled tilework as ornamentation dates back to the ancient civilizations of the Middle East.

stone blocks. The builders of Stonehenge probably used rollers or a sled. They may also have taken advantage of winter ice and snow to haul their loads.

Lack of machinery was compensated by the use of huge teams of workers, often forcibly recruited. The Early Egyptians developed a highly-sophisticated bureaucracy which, among other things, dealt with the recruitment and supervision of workers on the pyramids. Even more remarkable is the construction of the Great Wall of China. This fortification stretches across hundreds of miles of remote, inhospitable terrain. The workforce had to be maintained by a complex system of supply bases and transport columns.

When comparing the wonders of antiquity with those of more recent history it is interesting to see that religious faith frequently provided the inspiration for buildings of immense size or magnificence. The soaring medieval cathedral expresses the same spiritual fervour as the ziggurat or pyramid of much earlier cultures.

There are some man-made wonders which have been built for purely practical reasons. Warfare and subsequent necessity for self-defence has caused mankind, at various times, to build colossal fortresses, walled cities and great military barriers. Such marvels as the Great Wall of China, the impressive medieval castles of England and Wales or the lofty fortifications of an ancient town such as Carcassone in France, all possess their own rugged grandeur.

Civilizations which existed in an era of peace and harmony tended to produce wonders of elaborate beauty and luxury: whimsical gardens, ornate tombs, dazzling palaces and fairy-tale castles. Often such extravagances were built to glorify an individual ruler or religious leader. Ankor Wat in Cambodia, for example, was constructed to honour a semi-divine monarch; in the same way the sumptuous Palace of Versailles was built, centuries later, to flatter a French ruler.

Periods of stability and wealth also give rise to the cultivation of learning, scientific exploration and technical experiment. The Eiffel Tower and the

These fierce-looking temple guards stand watch in the Wat Phrakeo in Bangkok. The Wat Phrakeo is one of Thailand's most beautiful religious buildings and was built in 1784. It houses the world's most venerated Buddha image, which is made of green jasper and is known as the Emerald Buddha.

Pharos of Alexandria, although separated by 2000 years, were both built to demonstrate human achievements in the field of technology. Gustav Eiffel himself wrote that his tower was created 'to represent for all time the art of the engineer and the century of industry and science'.

At the root of every man-made wonder is Man's need to make order in his world and to justify his existence both to himself and to his gods.

When we look at the outstanding achievements of our own time, the marvels of this supremely inventive age are so numerous that we often tend to take them for granted. We see this century as somehow standing apart from all others in the history of mankind. The advances which man has made in the last few decades have been achieved at a speed which is almost frightening. Man's ingenious spirit and his constant desire to improve on his achievements have transformed the 20th century, perhaps more than any other, into an age of wonders.

We are daily surrounded by marvels of technology – vast supertankers, supersonic aircraft, skyscrapers, huge bridges, space vehicles, industrial machinery and computers – that we often cease to appreciate them as wonders. Far from going on pilgrimages to visit our own 'astounding sights' like the ancient Greeks, we accept each new marvel into our lives and rapidly learn to depend on it. Not only are today's wonders extremely numerous, but most of them are highly sophisticated and complex.

Although we may be impressed by the size of a tower-block or the streamlined grace of a jet aircraft, the great majority of us have only a vague appreciation of the organization, the minute planning and inventiveness which have created our modern marvels. Advanced technology and computer science are so specialized and complex that few of us are able to understand much more than the basic principles so that we tend to take for granted what we cannot understand.

Even though modern engineers and architects still seek to immortalize their skills, we now have more awareness of the impermanence of our creations. Of the original Seven Wonders of the World, only one, the Pyramids at Giza, has survived to the present day. Of the others, little remains except a few ruins and the occasional exquisite piece of sculpture. Ironically, the wonders of the past, designed to record the eternal supremacy of a particular empire or monarch, now serve in their ruined state to confirm the transience of all things created by mankind.

EGYPT AND THE NILE

Some of man's earliest architectural achievements are also among his greatest. The ancient Egyptians built their monuments to last for eternity and the vast pyramids at Giza, guarded by the Sphinx, have outlasted all the other Wonders of the ancient world.

Thebes was the great capital of Egypt during the period known as the New Kingdom (c. 1567 –1085 BC). The vast temples of Luxor (*below*) and Karnak (*right*) were dedicated to the supreme god Amon. Successive pharoahs paid homage to Amon in their massive building projects and strove to outdo their predecessors in their own additions to existing temples. Luxor was built by Amenhotep III in 1417 BC. It followed the usual plan of an Egyptian temple, having a sanctuary, an open courtyard and a colonnaded (hypostyle) hall. The huge columns shown are part of an additional courtyard that Amenhotep never completed. Further additions were made by Rameses II, the builder of Abu Simbel (see over page). Karnak was started by Thutmose I in about 1500 BC and was added to continuously until Roman times. Its great court covers an area of 8,919 square metres (10,600 square yards) and the famous Hypostyle Hall contains 134 huge columns. The largest of these are 21 metres (69 feet) in height and 10 metres (33 feet) thick. The colossal statue shown here stands in the Great Court at Karnak. It is the figure of a pharoah carved out of pink granite.

The rock temples of Abu Simbel (*below*) were built by Rameses II, another pharoah of the New Kingdom who reigned for 67 years. The temples are famous both as a spectacle and as the objects of a massive rescue operation undertaken some years ago. Because of a plan to build a reservoir and flood the area, these huge structures had to be removed from their original site and rebuilt on higher ground, set against a man-made mountain of concrete. This involved the transportation of 20,000 tons of rock. The Great Temple at Abu Simbel, with its four vast statues of Rameses, 20 metres (65 feet) in height, is dedicated to Amon and other major gods. The smaller temple shown here is dedicated to Hathor, the goddess of love and joy, and to Rameses' wife Nefertari. The six statues at the front are 10 metres (33 feet) high and represent Rameses and Nefertari.

The Step Pyramid at Saqqara (*right*) was built 100 years before those at Giza. It revolutionized tomb building in ancient Egypt and its shape heralds the straight-sided pyramids that were to come later. The earliest royal tombs were squat, rectangular structures called mastabas. Gradually the idea evolved that a more impressive building could be created by placing these mastabas one on top of the other in ever decreasing tiers. The Saqqara pyramid consists of six steps and is 61 metres (200 feet) high. It forms the focal point of a vast funeral complex or necropolis built for King Zoser in about 2760 BC. The man who built Saqqara, Imhotep, is the first architect to be named in history. The necropolis is especially important because it was the first structure in the world to be constructed entirely of square hewn stone rather than brick and wood.

ANCIENT GREECE AND ROME

The ideals of the Roman and Greek civilizations are stamped clearly on the marvels left behind. The great buildings of the Romans reveal their engineering genius, their pride and purposeful efficiency. The glories of Greece and above all the Parthenon (*below*), demonstrate the Greeks' love of beauty, harmony and proportion and their strong sense of citizenship

Ephesus (*left*) renowned for its temple of Artemis, one of the Seven Wonders of the World (see page 33), was also one of the most important cities of antiquity. It lies on the west coast of Asia Minor and was first colonized by Greeks in the 11th century BC.

Ephesus became wealthy and powerful, mainly because of its trade links and its importance as a place of pilgrimage. Even when it came under Roman domination from 190 BC onwards, Ephesus remained a glittering metropolis. The remains of houses, streets, libraries, gymnasia and theatres can still be seen. The ruins shown here are part of a triumphal arch, set up at the end of the 4th century AD and modelled on the Gate of Constantine in Rome.

These graceful female sculptures (*right*) known as caryatids, form part of the Erechtheion, one of the exquisite temples on the Acropolis at Athens. Acropolis means 'highest part of the city' and the sacred buildings now standing on it were begun at the command of Pericles in the middle of the 5th century BC. Towering over the city, the temples were designed to be an inspiration to the Athenian citizens. The Parthenon (see previous page) which was dedicated to Athena, is considered the most perfect Doric temple ever built. Its marvellous sculpture was the work of Phidias who also created the famous statue of Zeus at Olympia. The Erechtheion is in the Ionic style, its columns being more slender and ornate than those of the Parthenon. This little temple stands on what the Greeks believed was the most sacred part of the Acropolis and was dedicated to the heroes of Athens and to the Greek gods.

The theatre at Epidaurus (*right*) in the Peloponnesus is the best preserved and perhaps the most beautiful of all Greek theatres. Epidaurus was a popular and much visited religious sanctuary and consequently it had all the comforts expected of a sophisticated Greek city. The theatre with its 55 rows of white marble seats set into a hillside, was built by Polycletus in the 4th century BC. Greek drama evolved out of religious festivals held in honour of Dionysus, the god of wine and joy. The central circular area, called the orchestra, was occupied by the chorus who had an important role in early drama and commanded the most attention. The actors performed at the rear of the orchestra in front of scenery.

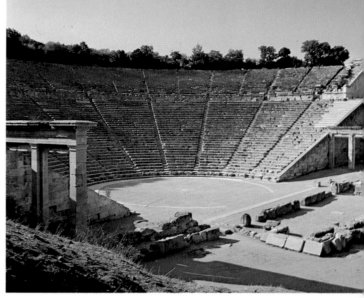

The Colosseum in Rome (*below*) is an amphitheatre which is regarded as one of the greatest architectural masterpieces of the Roman empire. It was built at the command of the emperor Vespasian and was completed in only six years by an unknown architect. The opening games were held there in AD 80 and the Colosseum was still being used for wild beast shows as late as AD 523. This vast arena which could seat a crowd of 48,000 was a gift of the Emperor to the Roman people. Vespasian wished to make himself and his family popular by giving the public the exciting spectacles which they loved. For 400 years the Colosseum was the scene of deadly gladiatorial fights, the mass slaughter of wild animals and the re-enactment of battles. The Colosseum was damaged several times by fire and earthquakes and during the Middle Ages it fell into disuse and was treated as a quarry.

The aqueducts at Nimes in the South of France (*left*) and at Segovia in Spain (*below*) demonstrate how the architecture of Imperial Rome was intended to be both functional and impressive. The aqueduct at Nimes, known as the Pont du Gard, is just one of the magnificent Roman remains which this city possesses. Nimes is also famous today for its superb Roman amphitheatre and the temple called the Maison Carrée (Square House). The Pont du Gard was built in 19 BC and has three tiers. The topmost tier is 548 metres (600 yards) long and 49 metres (160 feet) above the river. The aqueduct at Segovia has two tiers and contains 165 arches. It is built of huge granite blocks, without the use of mortar and is 813 metres (889 yards) long and 27 metres (90 feet) high. In AD 1072, 35 of its arches were destroyed by the Moors, but it was later restored in the 15th century and is still operating today.

FAMOUS CATHEDRALS

The style of church architecture in Western Europe has changed and developed a great deal over the centuries. By contrast, Eastern Orthodox churches have changed their shape very little since the early Christian period. The soaring Gothic cathedral of Mont St Michel (*below*), set dramatically on a rock off the coast of France, testifies to the glorious achievements of Christian architecture in the Middle Ages.

Detail of a stained glass window in Chartres Cathedral in France (*left*). From early Christian times, Chartres was a great centre of pilgrimage, having strong associations with the Virgin Mary. When an earlier church was virtually destroyed by fire in 1194, the citizens of Chartres eagerly organized the construction of a new cathedral, even harnessing themselves to carts to bring stone from the quarry. It took a mere 25 years to build Chartres as it stands today. Only its West façade and fine 12th century spire belong to the earlier church. Although Chartres contains a great deal of

superb sculpture, the most beautiful feature of the cathedral is its stained glass. The cathedral has 176 jewel-like windows mostly dating from the 13th century. The area of glass contained in these amounts to some 2,415 square metres (26,000 square feet).

The Cathedral of St Basil the Blessed (*below left*) in Moscow was built by order of Ivan the Terrible. This colourful cathedral, built of brick, consists of eight small chapels clustered round a central pyramid-like structure. There is a sinister legend that when St Basil's was completed in 1561 the Tzar had his craftsmen blinded to prevent them creating anything to rival his splendid cathedral. The distinctive onion-shaped domes are due to the fact that a conventional dome would collapse under the weight of winter snows.

These clustered, jagged spires (*below*) belong to the Sagrada Familia in Barcelona. This unfinished church is the work of the great Spanish architect Anton Gaudi (1852–1926). Gaudi was famed for the way his buildings reflected natural forms and textures.

The fine west façade of Lincoln Cathedral (*above*) is Norman, but the building mainly dates from the late 12th and 13th centuries. Its great central tower (hidden) is the tallest cathedral tower in England and measures 82.6 metres (271 feet).

It was early in the 16th century, when Julius II was Pope, that steps were finally taken to replace the old, decaying Church of St Peter in Rome with a new and magnificent basilica. This great triumph of the Renaissance period (*left*) took over 100 years to complete and during the construction of St Peter's, many men of genius contributed to its design: Bramante, Raphael, Michelangelo, Giocomo della Porta and finally Bernini who was responsible for much of the interior and the vast piazza in front of the church. Bramante created the original design for St Peter's, but its crowning glory, the great dome, must be attributed to Michelangelo who took over building operations in 1547. The dome is 138 metres (452 feet) above street level and is set on four massive piers, each 60 feet square. Unfortunately, Michelangelo did not live to see his design carried out.

TEMPLES AND MOSQUES

In the East are to be seen Islamic mosques and stone
Buddhist and Hindu temples adorned with sculpture. The
Taj Mahal at Agra in India is one of the great buildings of
Islam but is not a mosque. It is a marble mausoleum,
erected by the Indian Emperor Shah Jahan in 1653 for his
favourite wife.

The site on which the Dome of the Rock stands in Jerusalem (*below*) is, by an extraordinary trick of fate, sacred to Judaism, Christianity and to Islam. For nearly 2000 years Jerusalem and the Dome have been fought over by the followers of these three religions. The magnificent golden Dome was built in AD 687 by a Caliph, Abd al Malik, who wanted to make Jerusalem the spiritual centre of Islam rather than Mecca. The Dome is set directly over the sacred rock from which the prophet Muhammed is believed to have ascended into heaven. Abd al Malik employed the best Byzantine and Persian architects to build the shrine. He was so anxious that his monument should be just right that he made them build a smaller model of it first. This still stands today near the Dome of the Rock and is called the Dome of the Chain. The beautiful Persian tiles on the outside of the Dome were placed there in 1537 by Suleiman the Magnificent, the great Ottoman Sultan. The original Dome was covered with pure gold; now, sad to say, it is replaced with gilt aluminium.

Brilliant tilework decorates the Shaikh Lutfullah mosque in Isfahan (*right*). Shah Abbas of Persia (1587–1629) made Isfahan his new capital and during his lifetime transformed it into one of the world's loveliest cities. The principal buildings of Shah Abbas surround the central square or Maidan. They include the Royal and Lutfullah mosques and the Ali Qapu palace. In early Islamic buildings much of the tile decoration used was proper mosaic, each design made up of a mass of glazed fragments. From the 15th century, a cheaper method was adopted using square tiles which were already painted with part of the pattern. The Lutfullah, like the Royal mosque, contains both techniques.

This ornately carved doorway (*below left*) forms part of the immense temple complex of Ankor Wat in Cambodia. Ankor Wat is the most impressive of several hundred temples and monuments which lie in the dense Cambodian jungle. They are the work of the Khmers, the most brilliant civilization in South East Asia, which flourished between the 9th and 14th centuries. Ankor Wat itself was built in the 12th century as the dynastic shrine and mausoleum of the god-king Suryavarman II. The temple takes the form of a series of diminishing stone terraces. Its five great central towers signify the home of the Hindu gods. The chief glory of Ankor Wat is its marvellous bas reliefs which show mythological scenes and epic events.

The great temple-mountain at Borabadur (*below centre*) in Java dates from AD 800 and is a unique and outstanding creation of the Buddhist faith.

The Buddha shown was originally enclosed in a bell-shaped 'stupa' like those in the background. To Buddhists, the stupa is a symbol of eternal truth. Borabadur is covered with these and indeed forms a vast stupa itself. Carved out of a hill, Borabadur consists of a series of terraces, the walls of which are covered with stone reliefs revealing the teachings of Buddha. The temple contains an astonishing 5km (3 miles) of narrative carving. The temple-mountain is meant to be ascended by pilgrims who can meditate on the stone reliefs as they climb towards their goal, the central stupa.

At Bamiyan in northern Afghanistan is the world's most colossal statue of Buddha (*right*) carved out of a sandstone cliff. It is 53 metres (175 feet) tall and dates from the 3rd century AD. Another Buddha, 36·5 metres (120 feet) in height is close by.

SEVEN WONDERS OF THE WORLD

THE PYRAMIDS AT GIZA

The pyramids at Giza on the Nile were built during the period known as the Old Kingdom (c. 2900 – 2160 BC) when all Egypt was unified under a god-like king, the pharoah. The pyramids were built as royal tombs, designed to house the dead pharoah and all the comforts that his soul might require in the afterlife. Built for three 4th dynasty pharoahs, the Giza tombs of Cheops, Chephren and Mycerinus represent the finest achievements of the pyramid builders in ancient Egypt. During this period, skilled stone masons were permanently employed in the quarries along the Nile, cutting and shaping the limestone and granite blocks for the pyramids. These vast blocks, some weighing 70 tons or more, were brought by river from as far away as Aswan, 500 miles to the south of Giza.

Actual construction took place for only three months of every year, when the flooding of the Nile made agricultural work impossible. Thousands of peasants were then recruited to shift and position the stone blocks. The largest pyramid, that of Cheops, contains approximately 2,300,000 blocks and is still the most massive building in the world. Its square base measures 230 metres (755 feet) and before it lost its limestone outer casting, it was 146 metres (480 feet) high.

THE HANGING GARDENS OF BABYLON

Babylon was a wealthy city in Mesopotamia which reached the height of its power in about 600 BC. The luxurious Hanging Gardens, however, were the product of an earlier age; they were created by Queen Semiramis (c. 850 BC).

It is now thought likely that the Hanging Gardens were supported on the roof of large vaulted storehouses which were adjacent to the royal palace in Babylon. According to contemporary descriptions, the gardens grew on superimposed roof terraces, like the ascending levels of a Greek theatre – they only seem to have been 'hanging' in the sense that they were high above ground level.

The stone terraces were reinforced with bitumen reeds and sheets of lead to prevent damp seeping through. On top of this was a deep layer of mould which sustained the gardens. These took the form of a dazzling variety of tropical plants and fruit trees. In the intense dry heat of Mesopotamia, the luxuriance and beauty of so much cool greenery must have seemed marvellous indeed.

THE MAUSOLEUM OF HALICARNASSUS

Halicarnassus was a coastal town in Caria, a country lying in the south west of Asia Minor. The Mausoleum, a vast commemorative tomb, was commissioned for King Mausolus of Caria by his widow Artemisia, who was also his sister. Artemisia employed the best Greek sculptors and architects to work on the tomb which was completed in 351 BC. The Mausoleum was probably modelled on the tomb of the great King Cyrus of Persia. The Mausoleum was therefore a combination of Greek and Persian architecture, constructed according to the Greek laws of proportion and enriched with wonderfully sculpted friezes.

The tomb was 35 metres (115 feet) high and its base was 38 metres by 33 metres (127 feet by 108 feet). Its base was a six-stepped platform. Above this was a supporting stage, with two sculptured friezes; higher still was a peristyle of 36 Ionic columns surrounding the central shrine which also bore a frieze. Set on top of the columns was a step pyramid. This had a flat top to provide a platform for a marble chariot, drawn by four lifesize horses and containing the figures of Mausolus and Artemisia

THE COLOSSUS OF RHODES

Rhodes is an island off the south west coast of Asia Minor which was colonized by the Greeks and became an independent and prosperous power after the fall of the Alexandrian Empire. According to mythology, Rhodes was apportioned to the God of Light, Helios, as his share of the world: consequently, Helios was regarded by the Rhodians as their divine protector and patron. The Colossus was a huge statue of Helios, erected by the people of Rhodes in recognition of their god, who they believed had saved them from threatened invasion. The statue was set up somewhere in the harbour-city of Rhodes and probably served as a landmark for approaching ships.

The statue was 100 ft high and made of bronze hammered out in sections. The huge body was supported from the inside by a framework of iron and heavy stones. The Colossus is said to have taken 12 years to build and was finished in 290 BC. Sixty-six years later it was destroyed by an earthquake.

THE PHAROS OF ALEXANDRIA

The Pharos was a lighthouse, named after the island on which it stood in the harbour of Alexandria in Egypt. By the time the Pharos was built (279 BC) Alexandria had become an important, cosmopolitan port and a centre of science and learning.

Designed by Sostratus of Cnidus, the Pharos proved to be the archetype of all lighthouses. It consisted of three receding storeys. The lower section was four-sided and 71 metres (234 feet) high; this tapered slightly at the top and was surmounted by an octagonal storey. The third storey was 9 metres (30 feet) high and cylindrical in shape and contained the lighthouse fire. A large concave mirror reflected the light which, it was said, could be seen from a distance of 35 miles.

At the very top of the lighthouse was a colossal figure, possibly of Alexander the Great. The Pharos stood intact for many centuries but was finally converted into a mosque by the Turks in the 11th century.

THE STATUE OF ZEUS AT OLYMPIA

The famous statue of Zeus, the mightiest of the Greek gods, presided over the Olympic Games for over eight hundred years. It was housed in the great temple of Zeus at Olympia and on the eve of the games, each athlete came before the statue to swear an oath of honourable behaviour. The statue, completed in 433 BC, was the work of the renowned Greek sculptor, Phidias, whose masterpieces also decorated the Parthenon in Athens. It was 12 metres (40 feet) high, of Zeus seated on a throne raised up on a pedestal. On the pedestal were the figures of Greek deities. The statue was made of wood, but richly overlaid with ivory and gold.

THE TEMPLE OF ARTEMIS AT EPHESUS

The city of Ephesus was a Greek colony established on the west coast of Asia Minor. The Ephesians adopted the goddess Artemis as their special patroness and built in her honour the largest and most magnificent temple the world had ever seen. The cult of Artemis, the Mother-Goddess of Nature, was one of great antiquity. The Artemision, as the temple was called, followed the usual Greek style of a peristyle surrounding the central shrine or cella. The 127 columns round the shrine were almost 20 metres (65 feet) high. The temple itself measured 126 metres by 65 metres (413 feet by 214 feet). The 36 sculptured columns were probably located at the front of the building. The sculpture formed a decorative frieze round the lower part of each column and depicted stories of the gods and heroes.

WONDERS OF THE WILDERNESS

Many highly developed cultures of the past, which have ceased to exist, have left us awesome evidence of their original glory. The great civilizations of central America are typical; these sculptured columns (*below*) once supported the roof of a temple at Tula, the ancient capital of the Toltecs who flourished in Mexico during the 11th century AD.

This strange, eerie stone face (*above*) is one of many to be seen on remote Easter Island in the Pacific Ocean. Today, Easter Islanders can remember almost nothing about their ancestors who quarried and set up these great statues. There are well over 600 statues or *moai* on the island, some of them weighing many tons. One of the largest weighs 82 tons and was transported four miles from the quarry. It is thought that these faces were set up to commemorate illustrious ancestors, and that a violent civil war among the islanders brought the making of *moai* to a sudden end.

Machu Picchu (*left*) a fortress city high in the Peruvian Andes was built by the Incas, a great civilization destroyed by the Spanish Conquistadores in 1532. The Incas were builders with extraordinary skill although they had no iron tools and no knowledge of the wheel. Machu Picchu was discovered in 1911.

WALLS, BRIDGES AND STRONGHOLDS

For centuries Man resorted to massive fortifications to protect himself from his enemy. Even though the need for strongholds has now gone we are still fascinated by the imposing splendour of the great fortress. Penrhyn Castle, in Wales (*below*), was built in the last century when Norman-style castles were fashionable.

The massive walls and turrets of the city of Carcassonne in southern France (*left*) date, in part, from Roman times. The fortifications also contain the work of the Visigoths, Germanic barbarians who held Carcassonne in the 5th century. Throughout its history, Carcassonne has had the reputation of being an unassailable fortress. Charlemagne unsuccessfully laid siege to it in the 9th century. The story goes that a certain Dame Carcas of the city, from whom it takes its name, saved the starving inhabitants by feeding a pig with the last of her corn in full view of the attacking army. Charlemagne's troops withdrew, thinking that the citizens had plenty of provisions.

The Great Wall of China (*above*) is the longest man-made structure in the world. The main wall is 3460km (2150 miles) in length but additional spurs and branches add up to a further 2864km (1780 miles). The wall ranges in height from 4.5 to 12 metres (15 to 39 feet) and is up to 9 metres (32 feet) thick. The main wall as it appears today dates from the Ming dynasty (14th–17th century) when it was extensively rebuilt. However, it was originally built by the first Emperor of China in the 3rd century BC. He constructed a wall 2897 metres (1800 miles) in length along his northern border to keep out marauding nomads. It incorporated many existing fortifications.

Bridges

Tower Bridge on the river Thames (*above*) is the most distinctive and best known of London's bridges. It was built between 1886 and 1894 and its central section between the Gothic towers is designed to split in half to allow large vessels through. It takes 1.5 minutes to raise the two drawbridges which each weigh 1,000 tons. The original steam pumping engines which provided the hydraulic power to raise the bridge have now been replaced by electric motors.

The Sydney Harbour Bridge in Australia (*above left*), built in 1932, is the world's widest, long-span bridge. The bridge is 48 metres (160 feet) wide and carries two railway tracks and eight lanes of traffic. The top of its arch is 134 metres (440 feet) above sea level.

The Golden Gate (*left*) in San Francisco harbour was for many years the longest suspension bridge in the world. With its reddish gold frame and slender supporting cables it is still one of the most beautiful bridges. The bridge is nearly 2.4 km (1.5 miles) long and was opened in 1936. It stands as a monument to the courage of its builders who constructed the bridge despite the dangerous currents which sweep in and out of the harbour.

GREAT PALACES

The fairy-tale palace of Neuschwanstein looks like the
stronghold of a medieval knight, but was only built in the
mid-19th century. It was created by Ludwig II, the mad
king of Bavaria, who lived in a world of fantasy and legends.
The palace has a throne room in the Byzantine style and
even an artificial grotto complete with stalactites.

The chateau of Villandry in France (*left*) is famous for its formal gardens, laid out in the 16th-century style. The box borders of flower beds form a maze of precise geometrical patterns.

The Escorial Palace near Madrid (*below*) was built by the devout Spanish king, Philip II. It is a strange combination of royal residence, monastery and place of learning. Completed in 1584, it covers an area of 37,164 square metres (400,000 square feet) and contains 16 court-yards, 1200 doors and 2673 windows.

The magnificent ceiling (*right*) of the Salon d'Hercule at the palace of Versailles in France is painted on a single, enormous canvas and took the artist three years to complete. Versailles, as famous for its splendid, whimsical pleasure grounds as for the palace itself, was begun in 1661 by Louis XIV, the Sun King. The gardens were laid out by the great landscape architect, Le Notre. For nearly 130 years, until the Revolution in 1789, Versailles was both the playground and the seat of power of the French monarchy.

Chenonceaux (*above*) is one of the famous chateaux of the Loire Valley in France. The turreted wing, seen on the left, is the oldest part, dating from the early 16th century. At one time Chenonceaux belonged to the kings of France. Henry II gave it to his mistress, Diane de Poitiers, who built the bridge across the river. However, the lovely Classical gallery on the bridge was built by Henry's widow, Catherine de Medici.

The Doge's Palace in Venice (*left*) stands next to St Mark's cathedral. With its delicate, lace-like stonework and façade of pink and white marble, this beautiful building bears the stamp of both Eastern and Western influences. It seems the embodiment of the wealth, luxury and power of Venice at the height of her prosperity. In its present form, the palace dates from the 14th and 15th centuries. One of its striking external features are the wonderful stone carvings on the capitols of the lower porticos and at the corners of the building. The palace was the official dwelling place of the Doge who was the chief magistrate in Venice. Here, too, the supreme judges of the city met in council. The public rooms of the palace are sumptuously decorated with paintings by famous Renaissance artists such as Veronese, Tiepolo and Tintoretto. Within the palace is a magnificent staircase, which is elaborately decorated with gilded stucco and called the Scala d'Oro (Golden Staircase).

The magnificent palace of Schönbrunn (*above*) with its warm yellow façade is set in beautiful French-style gardens on the outskirts of Vienna. It was built during the reign of the Empress Maria Theresa (1740–60). Originally the Empress wanted her summer palace to rival Versailles, but the grandiose design of the famous architect, Fischer von Erlach, was never fully realized. However, Schönbrunn with its 1200 rooms has had as momentous a history as any other great palace – Mozart came to entertain the court here as a child of six, Marie Antoinette spent her childhood here, and Napoleon used the palace as his headquarters in 1805 and 1809.

This shimmering white marble palace (*above*) is set on an island on the Pichola lake at Udaipur in India. In fact the island contains a collection of palaces dating from the 17th century and built by the rulers of Mewar state. Such display of wealth and luxury was typical of Indian princes wishing to assert their independence.

Two ceremonial halls in the Forbidden City (*left*), the old Imperial Palace in Peking. Covering an area of about 101 hectares (250 acres) it is the largest palace in the world. It was built in the 15th century by the Emperor Yung-Lo. For 500 years China was ruled from the Forbidden City.

Matsumato (*right*), one of Japan's most elegant castles, dates from 1587. Like almost all Japanese buildings, it is primarily made of wood to allow for earthquakes.

HISTORICAL LANDMARKS

Throughout history, Man has created monuments. One of his most impressive achievements must be the four portraits of American presidents, carved in a granite cliff in Dakota.

The Statue of Liberty (*left*) one of the best-known landmarks in the world, stands at the entrance to New York harbour on a small island. In 1865, it was decided that the French nation should give a statue to the Americans to commemorate the alliance between France and the United States during the American War of Independence. In 1874, a sculptor, Frédéric-Auguste Bartholdi, began to design the statue. The vast, steel framework of the statue was designed by Gustav Eiffel, the great French engineer who was to build the Eiffel Tower. The figure itself consisted of 300 hammered copper plates applied to the framework. Meanwhile, the Americans were preparing the pedestal for the statue on Bedloe's island in New York harbour. In 1885, the Statue of Liberty was shipped over to America in dismantled sections. It represents a crowned woman, the Goddess of Liberty, who is holding aloft a symbolic torch and carrying the Declaration of Independence. The figure is an astonishing size; it weighs a total of 225 tons and the symbolic torch is 93 metres (305 feet) above sea level. The head of the statue measures 3.5 metres by 5 metres (10 feet by 17 feet). The raised arm is 13 metres (42 feet) in length, and 3.6 metres (12 feet) in diameter.

This fine skyscraper (*above left*), the Transamerica Pyramid in San Francisco, stands as a monument to modern architectural achievement. It is an example of how contemporary architects have learnt to develop the potential of a high-rise building, giving it its own style and beauty. The Transamerica Pyramid is 260 metres (853 feet) high and has 48 storeys.

A famous monument to the fallibility of Man is the leaning Tower of Pisa in Italy (*above right*) The tower began to lean when it was only 9 metres (30 feet) high because its foundations began to sink. This beautiful Romanesque building with its eight storeys of rounded arches, is in fact a bell tower or campanile. It was begun in 1173 but was not completed until about 1305. Throughout the 13th century, efforts were made to correct the tower's inclination as building proceeded, but all was to no avail and eventually it was finished at a height of 55 metres (180 feet). The great physicist and astronomer, Galileo (1564–1642), who was a native of Pisa, used the leaning tower for his experiments with falling objects. The tower now leans 4 metres (14 feet) out of perpendicular and this is increasing fractionally each year.

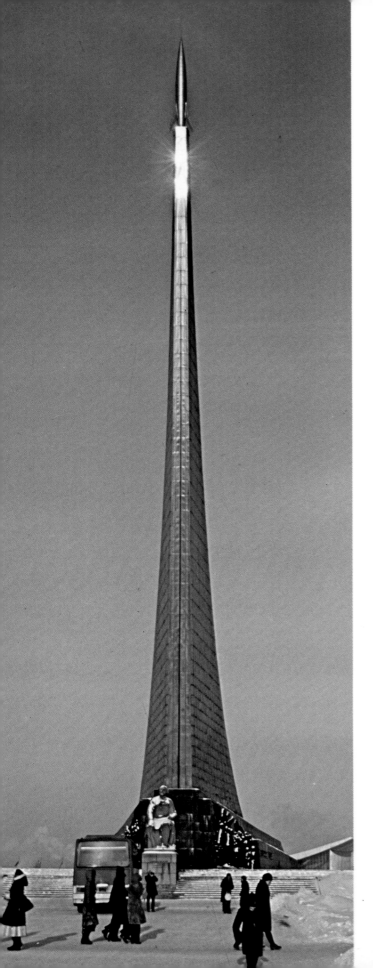

The Expodus in Moscow (*left*) was set up to commemorate the progress of the Soviet people in their exploration of outer space. This silvery shaft soars up to a height of 95 metres (313 feet) and was unveiled in 1964. The monument consists of a steel frame faced with sheets of polished titanium. On both sides of its granite base are sculptures depicting people past and present engaged in space exploration.

The massive steel framework of the Eiffel Tower (*right*) looms up into the darkness. This extraordinary feat of engineering has come to be one of the great symbols of Paris. It was built by Gustav Eiffel for the Paris Exhibition of 1889 and was intended to demonstrate the possibilities of modern steel construction. Just over 305 metres (1000 feet) high, the Tower was the tallest skyscraper of its day. Since 1918 the Tower has been used as a transmitting station for French radio.

The strange outline of the Atomium (*below*) dominates the park of Laeken in Brussels. It was built as a symbol of the World Fair which was held in Brussels in 1958. The Atomium, which is made of steel-coated aluminium, represents an atom of iron, the nine spheres being the electrons. It stands nearly 122 metres (400 feet) high and each sphere is 1768 metres (58 feet) in diameter. The spheres can be reached by escalator and three of them contain exhibitions on the peaceful use of nuclear energy.

MODERN MARVELS

Many of our modern wonders are essentially functional, designed to conserve space, create new sources of energy or make travel faster and easier. Yet the magnificent opera house in Sydney Harbour, Australia is proof that the technological age can still create beauty for its own sake. The white, sail-like roof vaults serve a purely decorative purpose and are a breathtaking ornament to Sydney's waterfront.

Surely one of the best-known skylines in the world is that of Manhattan Island in New York (*above*), the home of the skyscraper. The island of Manhattan was sold by the Indians to European settlers for a few dollars. Ironically, it is the enormous value of land on Manhattan in modern times that has led to the construction of high-rise buildings. The huge population increase at the turn of the century and the revolutionary method of construction using a steel frame were two other reasons for their development. The first skyscrapers appeared in the 1920s. The Empire State building (*extreme left*) was completed in 1932 and with its 102 storeys was for 50 years the world's tallest building. Now it is dwarfed by the twin towers of the World Trade Center (*extreme right*) which is the largest office building in the world and the highest skyscraper in New York. The taller of the two towers is 411 metres (1,350 feet) high.

The Hoover Dam on the Colorado river in the United States (*top right*) was built in 1936 and was for 22 years the world's highest dam. It is 221 metres (726 feet) high and is made of concrete. It is an arch-gravity dam which means that both its own weight and its inward curve help the dam to resist the pressure of water. A large number of dams have been built in recent years as large reservoirs are now an important source of hydroelectric power.

The most complex interchange in the British road system at Gravelly Hill, near Birmingham (*above*), is popularly known as Spaghetti Junction. It is an example of how modern engineering avoids a potential bottleneck where several major roads meet. Spaghetti Junction consists of 18 routes on 6 levels and includes a diverted river and canal. It consumed 250,000 tons of concrete, 300,000 tons of earth and 26,000 tons of steel, and cost £8m to build.

Skylab (*left*) was the space laboratory which was launched into the Earth's orbit by the Americans in 1973. It was made out of hardware left over from the Apollo project, the great enterprise which took men to the Moon in 1969. Skylab proved an outstanding success as a means of carrying out experiments and long-term surveys in space. It was occupied for a total of 315 days, the men being transported in Apollo-type spacecraft. The last crew stayed in Skylab for 84 days.

Off-shore rigs like this one in the Persian Gulf (*right*) tap the vast oil fields which lie beneath the sea. Their role is vital in today's world where oil is the primary source of energy.